BELLWETHER MEDIA • MINNEAPOLIS, MN

Blastoff! Readers are carefully developed by literacy experts to build reading stamina and move students toward fluency by combining standards-based content with developmentally appropriate text.

Level 1 provides the most support through repetition of high-frequency words, light text, predictable sentence patterns, and strong visual support.

Level 2 offers early readers a bit more challenge through varied sentences, increased text load, and text-supportive special features.

Level 3 advances early-fluent readers toward fluency through increased text load, less reliance on photos, advancing concepts, longer sentences, and more complex special features.

★ **Blastoff! Universe**

Reading Level

Grade K

Grades 1–3

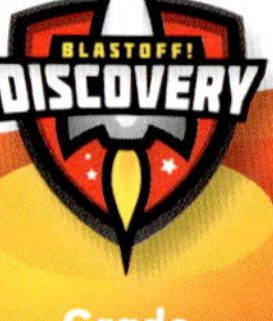

Grade 4

This edition first published in 2023 by Bellwether Media, Inc.

Library of Congress Cataloging-in-Publication Data

LC record for See Corn Grow available at http://lccn.loc.gov/2022039504

Editor: Betsy Rathburn Designer: Brittany McIntosh

Printed in the United States of America, North Mankato, MN.

Table of Contents

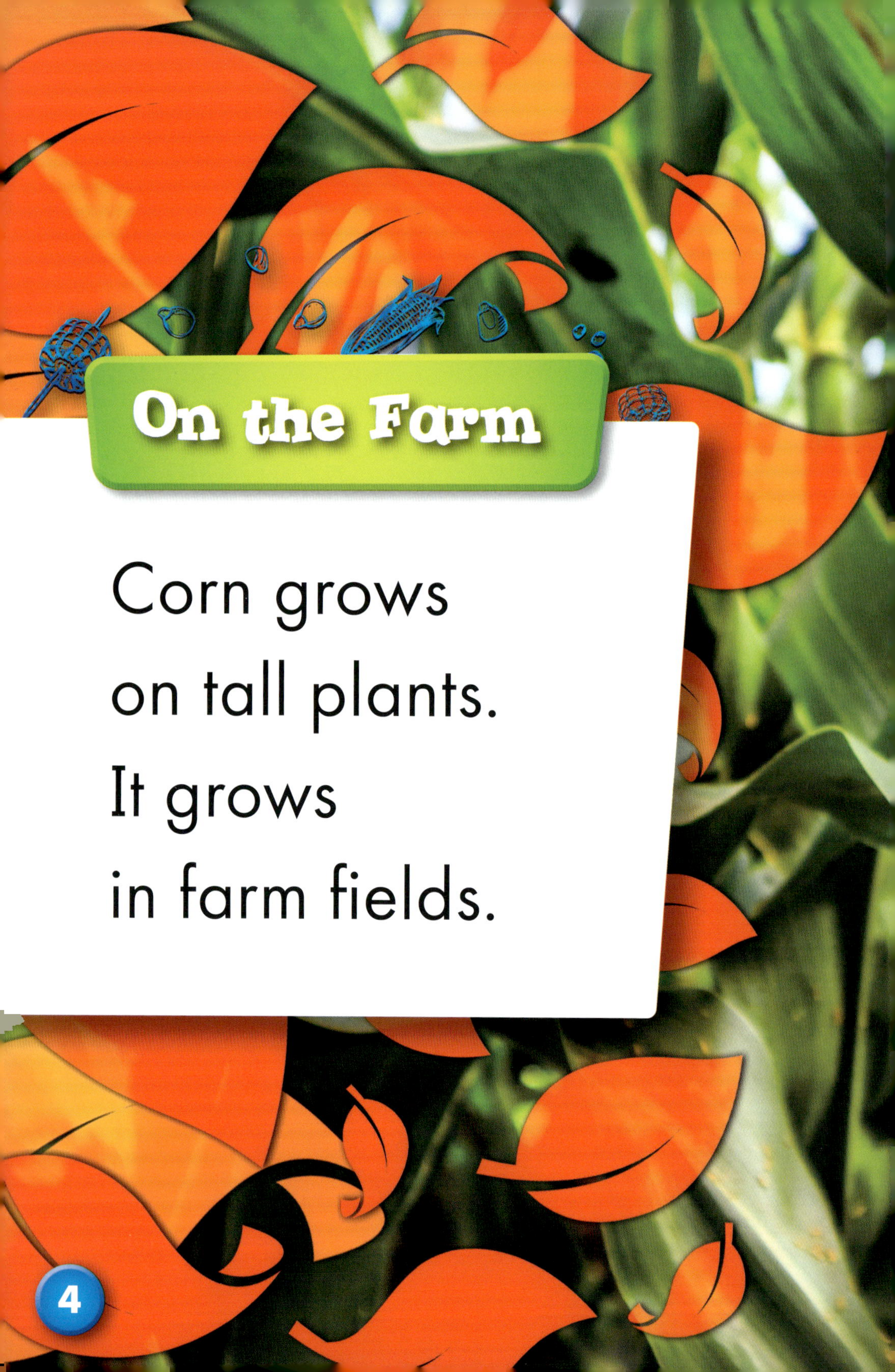

On the Farm

Corn grows
on tall plants.
It grows
in farm fields.

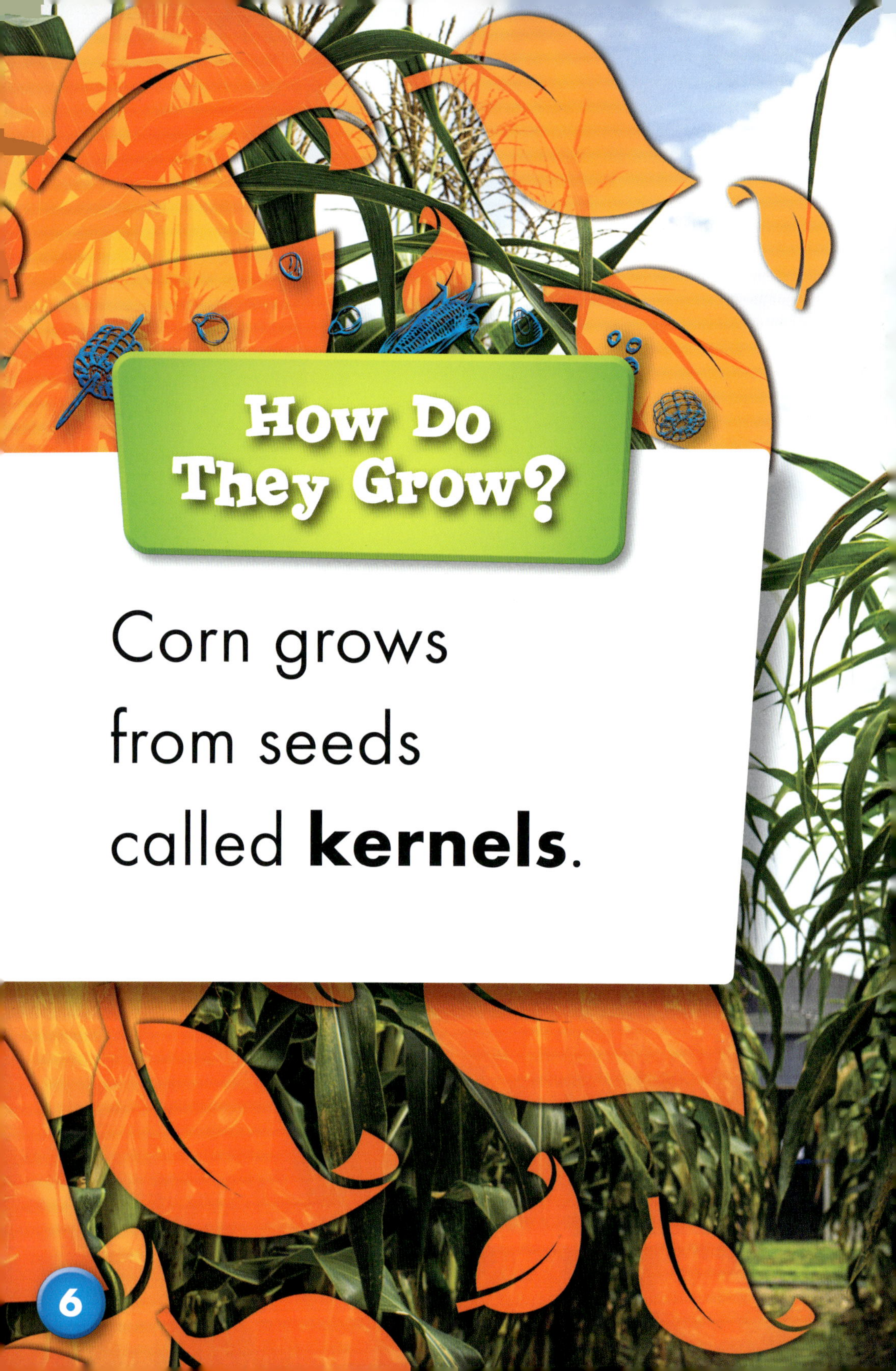

How Do They Grow?

Corn grows from seeds called **kernels**.

kernels

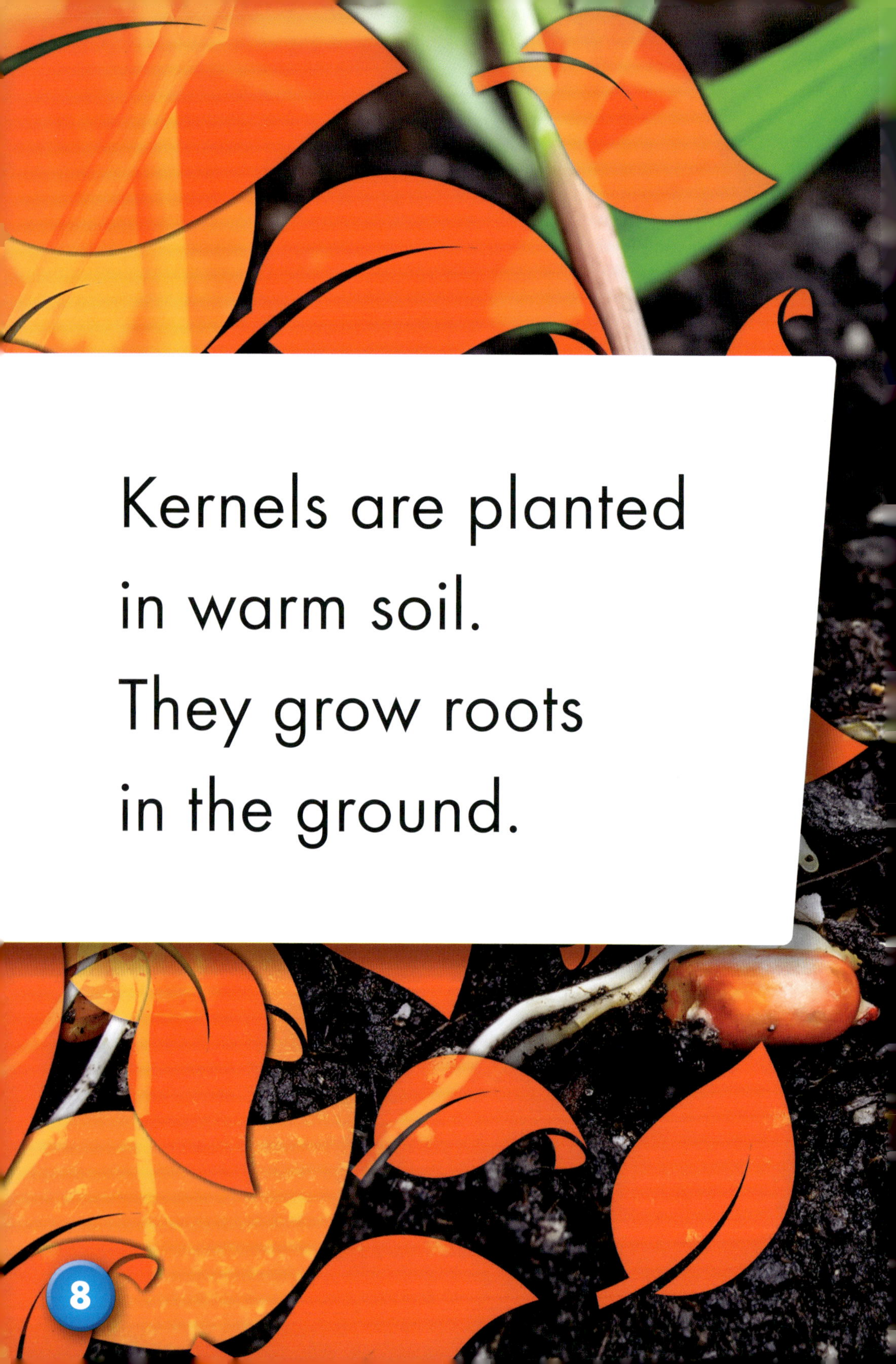

Kernels are planted in warm soil. They grow roots in the ground.

roots

A small plant
pokes out
of the ground.
It becomes
a tall **stalk**.

Needed to Grow
warm soil
wind
water
stalk

Tassels grow
at the top
of the stalk.
They let out **pollen**.

tassel
pollen

Wind blows
the pollen.
It lands on
the plant's **silk**.

silk

Each piece of silk grows a kernel. The kernels form an ear. A **husk** covers each ear.

ear
husk

Fully Grown

One or two ears grow on each stalk. Farmers gather them.

Using Corn
popcorn
corn
on the cob
cereal
gathering
corn
CLAAS

We pull off
the husks.
We are having
corn for dinner!

Corn Life Cycle
1
kernels are planted in warm soil
2
kernels form roots and grow into stalks
3
stalks grow tassels that let out pollen
4
pollen lands on silk and kernels grow

Glossary

husk

the leaves that cover an ear of corn

silk

strings that grow kernels on an ear of corn

kernels

seeds that grow on an ear of corn

stalk

the long, skinny part of a plant

pollen

a powder made by some plants that lets them grow seeds

tassels

the parts of a corn plant where pollen forms

To Learn More

AT THE LIBRARY

Brannon, Cecelia H. *Corn.* New York, N.Y.: Enslow Publishing, 2018.

Nelson, Robin. *The Story of Corn: It Starts With a Seed.* Minneapolis, Minn.: Lerner Publications, 2021.

Sterling, Charlie W. *Corn.* Minneapolis, Minn.: Jump!, 2023.

ON THE WEB

FACTSURFER

Factsurfer.com gives you a safe, fun way to find more information.

1. Go to www.factsurfer.com.
2. Enter "see corn grow" into the search box and click 🔍.
3. Select your book cover to see a list of related content.

Index

The images in this book are reproduced through the courtesy of: xpixel, front cover (kernel); Krumao, front cover (seedling); Kovaleva_Ka, front cover (corn), p. 3; Kwangmoozaa, pp. 4-5; TB studio, pp. 6-7; ELAKSHI CREATIVE BUSINESS, p. 7 (top); Oleksandr Yuchynskyi, pp. 8-9; ShaduraViktor, pp. 10-11; Antonio Gravante, p. 11 (top left); Anirut Thailand, p. 11 (top middle); amenic181, p. 11 (top right); Alena Stalmashonak, pp. 12-13; Fir Mamat/ Alamy, pp. 13 (bottom), 22 (pollen); Tritanee, pp. 14-15; Aedka Studio, pp. 16-17; Photoagriculture, pp. 18-19; M. Unal Ozmen, p. 19 (top left); vvoe, p. 19 (top middle); goffkein.pro, p. 19 (top right); Nikkikii, pp. 20-21; lovelyday12, p. 22 (husk); Evan Lorne, p. 22 (kernels); Vietnam Stock Images, p. 22 (silk); Svend77, p. 22 (stalk); rootstock, p. 22 (tassels); Spalnic, p. 23.